STORYBOOK SKILLS

STORYBOOK LETTERS

by Marilynn G. Barr

Publisher: Roberta Suid

Production: Little Acorn & Associates, Inc.

MM2205
STORYBOOK LETTERS
Entire contents copyright © 2005
by Monday Morning Books, Inc.

For a complete catalog, write to the address below:
Monday Morning Books, Inc.
PO Box 1134
Inverness, CA 94937

Call our toll-free number: 1-800-255-6049
E-mail us at: MMBooks@aol.com
Visit our Web site:
http://www.mondaymorningbooks.com
For more products featuring art by Marilynn G. Barr visit www.littleacornbooks.com

ISBN 1-57612-257-3

Printed in the United States of America
9 8 7 6 5 4 3 2 1

Contents

Introduction

Storybook Letters is one of four books in the Storybook Skills series. From the storybook classic *Corduroy* to favorite fables such as "Jack and the Beanstalk," exciting projects and activities introduce and reinforce letter recognition and pre-reading skills. In hands-on activities such as "Overalls for Bears" and "Toy Box Alphabet," children match uppercase and lowercase letters. Children place alphabet-programmed blueberries in a jar after reading Caldecott Honor book *Blueberries for Sal*.

Activities may be used with a variety of different storybooks. Children can make blueberry pie pictures after reading *Blueberry Mouse*, or color calico cats after reading *Millions of Cats*.

Cards and patterns can also be used in a variety of ways. More advanced students can practice alphabetizing with the different ABC patterns found in the book and the ABC picture cards found on the bottom of this page. Patterns can be enlarged and used to decorate bulletin boards or displays. Children can use patterns to make alphabet-themed art projects. Or write messages on the patterns and use as reward certificates.

From A to Z, *Storybook Letters* provides an abundance of alphabet-skills practice!

Alphabet Pictures

Alphabet Blueberry Pails

Reproduce, color, and cut out blueberries and 26 pails. Tape two large sheets of construction paper along both sides of the short ends. Fold each side in half towards the taped center. Then fold along the taped center in the opposite direction to form an accordion folder. Attach an envelope to the back to store blueberries. Decorate, then write "Alphabet Blueberry Pails" on the front of the folder. Program each pail with an uppercase letter and each blueberry with a lowercase letter. Unfold the accordion and glue the pails inside. To practice alphabet skills, children place matching lowercase blueberries on uppercase pails.

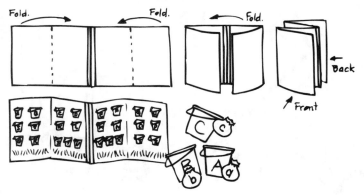

Alphabet Bears

Reproduce and program 26 sets of baby and momma bear patterns (p. 7) with upper and lowercase letters. Laminate and cut apart the bears for children to match. Decorate, then write "Alphabet Bears" on the front of a large envelope. Children can work individually or in small groups to match upper and lowercase letters. For additional letter skills practice, reproduce, color, cut out, and glue alphabet pictures on 26 additional bear patterns.

Blueberries in a Jar

Provide each child with a set of alphabet pictures, a sheet of construction paper, and a clear storage bag. Enlarge and reproduce three blank blueberry cards for each child to color and cut out along the bold lines. Have children write an upper and matching lowercase letter on two of the blueberries. Then have them color, cut out, and glue the matching alphabet picture (p. 4) on the third blueberry. Have children glue their berries close together in the center of a sheet of construction paper. Place a plastic storage bag over each child's berries, then use a permanent marker to draw a jar shape around the berries. Help children cut out and glue their jar shapes over their blueberries. Children can cut and glue construction paper lids at the tops of their jars. Trim the construction paper around each child's jar, then write his or her name on the back.

Blueberry Pie, Anyone?

Draw an eight-space grid on four separate sheets of paper, then program each grid square with an upper or lowercase letter of the alphabet. Reproduce each letter grid and a set of blueberry pies for each child to decorate, color, and cut out. Provide children with envelopes to store their grids and blueberry pies. Working with one grid at a time, children place pies with matching alphabet pictures on the letter spaces on the grids.

Girl and Mother

Provide children with craft sticks, crayons, markers, scissors, and glue to make stick puppets.

Baby Bear and Momma Bear

Provide children with craft
sticks, crayons, markers,
scissors, and glue to make
stick puppets.

Blueberries

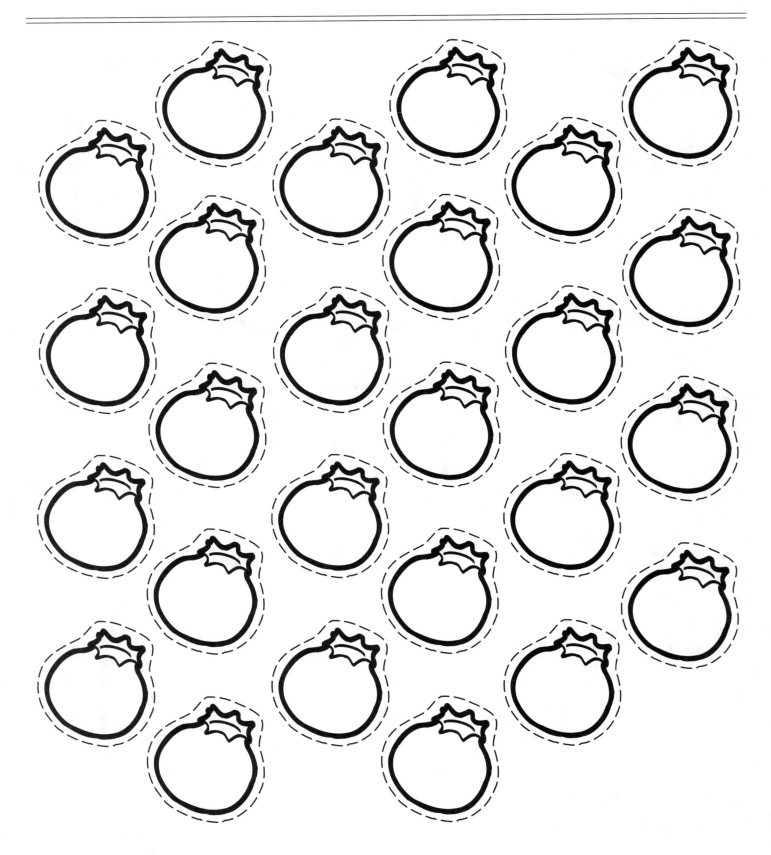

Prepare a work station with construction paper blueberries, crayons, markers, scissors, yarn, and glue for children to make blueberry necklaces.

Pails

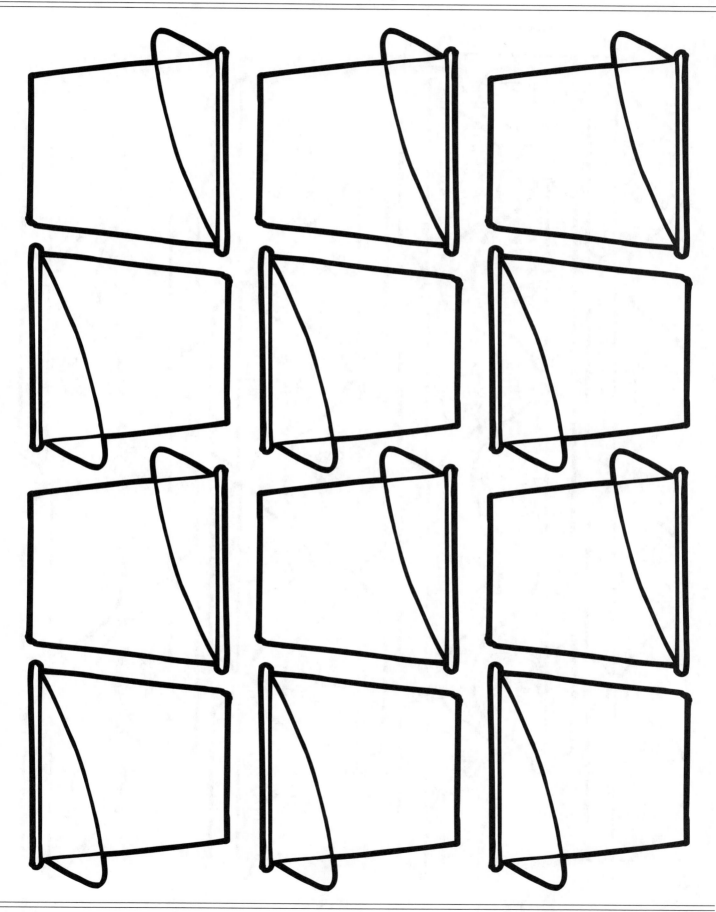

9

Blueberry Pies

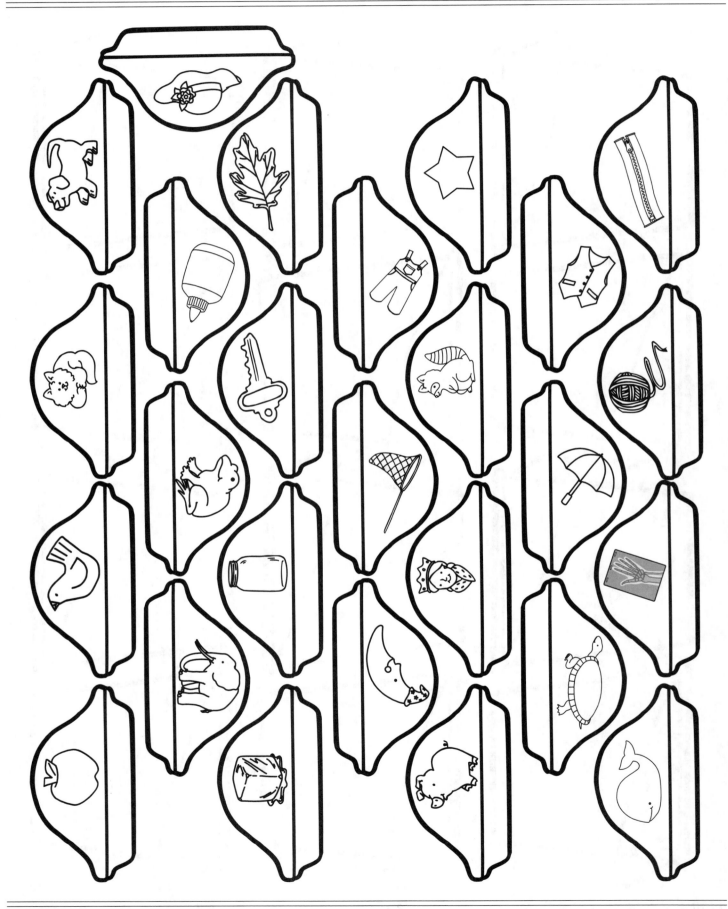

Let's Play *Journey Over Blueberry Hill*

Assembly

Reproduce, color, and cut out the "Journey Over Blueberry Hill" game board patterns. Matching in the center, glue the game board patterns on a sheet of oak tag. Decorate the border around the game board, then laminate. Reproduce, color, laminate, then cut out the pawns and two sets of game cards. Measure, cut, and tape a construction paper pocket to the back of the game board for pawn and game card storage.

To Play

Set up the game board on a table. Shuffle and place the game cards, face down, next to the game board. Each player, in turn, draws a card and moves his or her pawn to the space with the matching letter. Players place used cards in a discard pile. When all cards have been drawn, reshuffle the discard pile for children to continue playing. Play continues until each player reaches The End.

Pawns

Journey Over Blueberry Hill Game Board

The End

Journey Over Blueberry Hill Game Cards

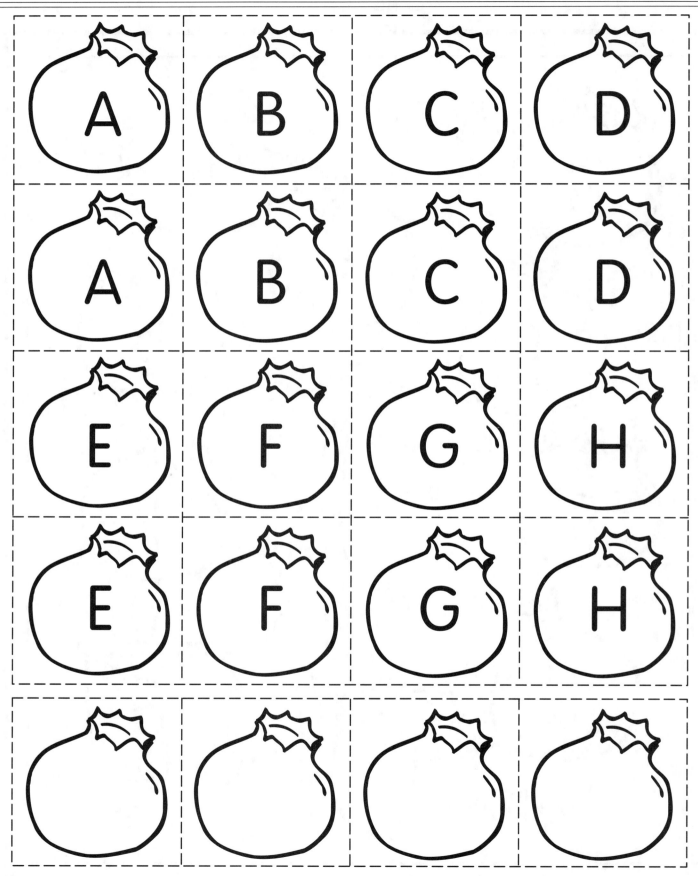

Reprogram game board and cards with alternate sets of letters for additional letter recognition skills practice.

Overalls For Bears

Reproduce and color 26 bears and overalls. Program each bear and a pair of overalls with matching upper and lowercase letters. Laminate and cut out the programmed bears and overalls. Decorate and write "Overalls For Bears" on the front of an envelope to store bears and overalls. Children can work individually or in small groups to place overalls on matching bears. For more alphabet skills practice, reproduce, color, and glue alphabet pictures on 26 additional overalls. Then laminate for children to match to the correct letter bears.

Toy Box Alphabet

Provide each child with a folder and a toy box pattern to decorate. Program and reproduce toy cards with upper and lowercase letters for each child. Write "Toy Box Alphabet" and each child's name on the front of his or her folder. Have children glue their toy boxes to the inside of their folders. Provide envelopes for children to tape to the backs of folders. Children can practice alphabet skills by sorting and matching all of the uppercase toys or lowercase toys on their toy boxes.

Alphabet Patchwork Overalls

Enlarge and reproduce a pair of oak tag overalls (p. 17) for each child to color and cut out. Measure and cut construction paper patches to fit on the overalls and place them in a bowl at a work station. Have children write matching upper and lowercase letters on patches to glue on their overalls. Mount each child's "Alphabet Patchwork Overalls" on a sheet of construction paper.

Bear's Buttons

Each child will need a file folder, a bear pattern (p. 16), an envelope, and a set of oak tag alphabet buttons. Have children color, cut out, and glue bear patterns to the fronts of their folders. Write "Bear's Buttons" and each child's name on the front of his or her folder. Have children color and cut apart their buttons. Provide children with envelopes to tape to the backs of their folder to store buttons. Children will use the folders as a display case to match bear's upper and lowercase button collection.

15

Bears

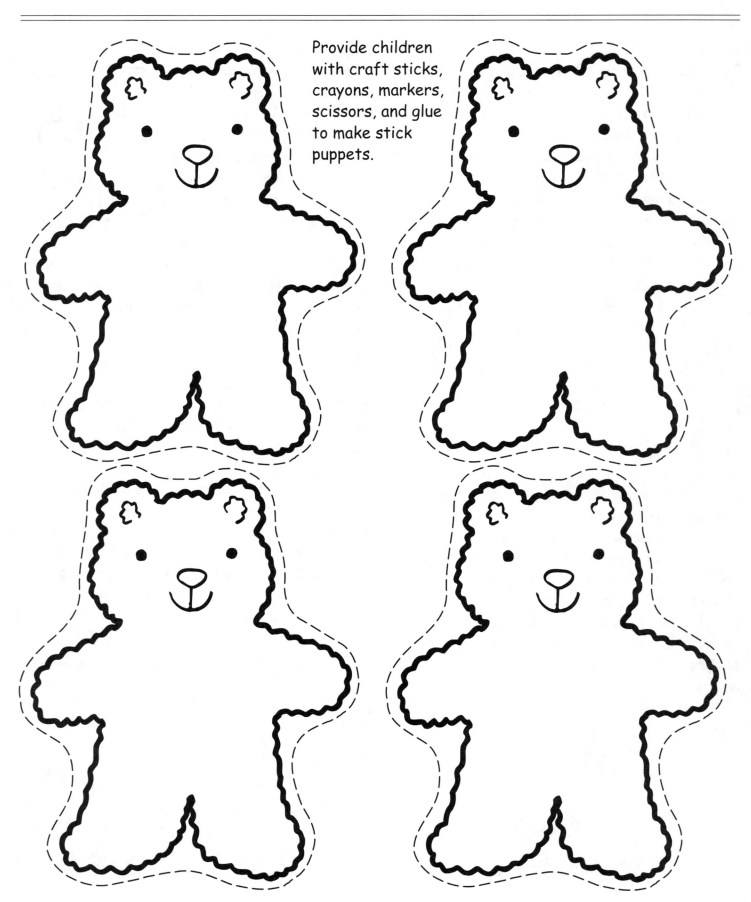

Provide children with craft sticks, crayons, markers, scissors, and glue to make stick puppets.

Overalls

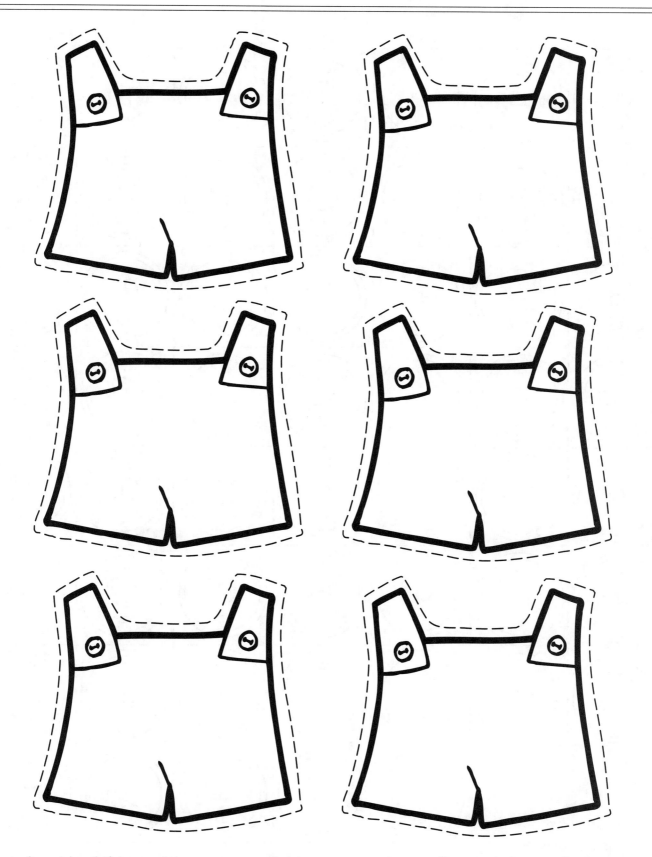

Provide children with crayons and scissors to make a collection of overalls for their stick puppets. Children can fasten the overalls to bears with paper clips.

Alphabet Buttons

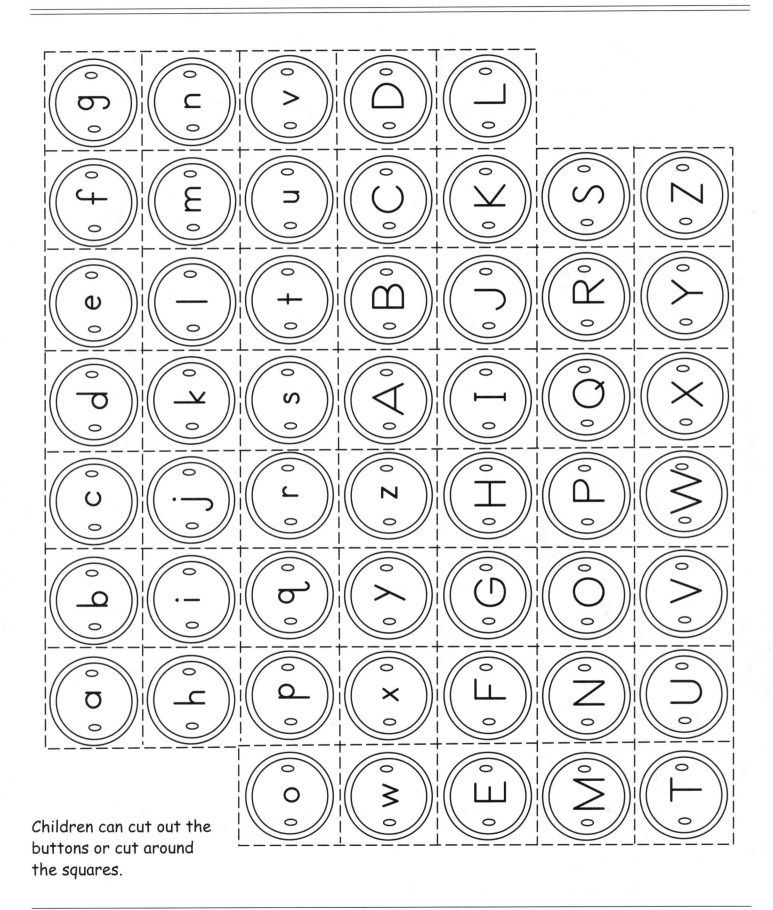

Children can cut out the buttons or cut around the squares.

Toy Box

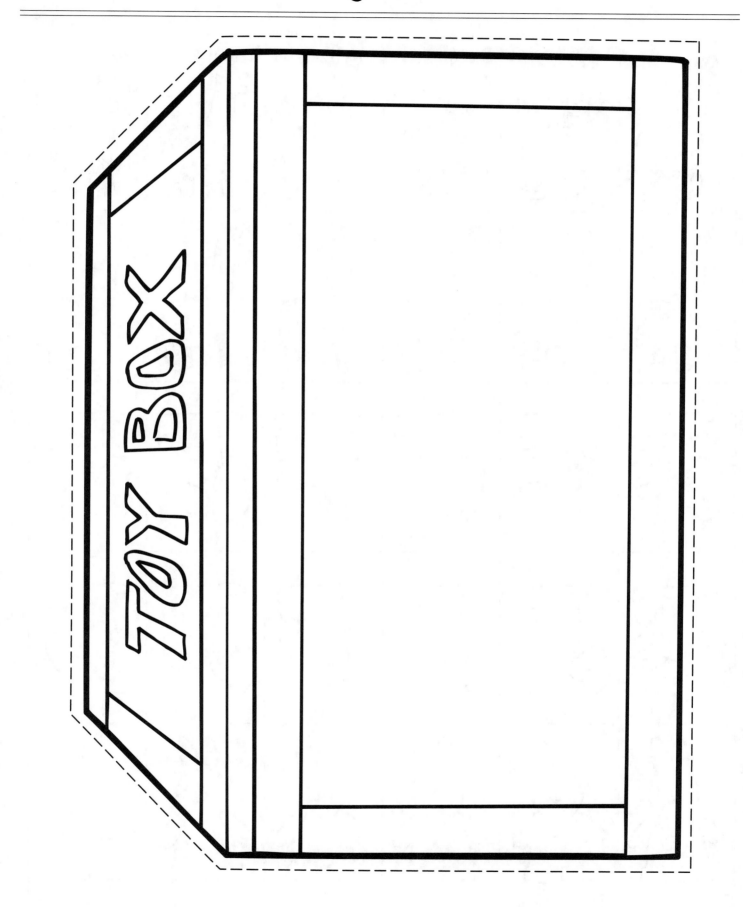

Toy Cards

Toy Cards

Let's Play *Find Bear's Buttons*

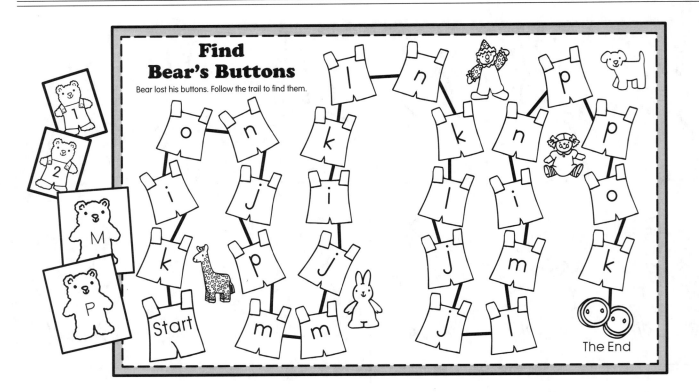

Assembly

Reproduce, color, and cut out the "Find Bear's Buttons" game board patterns. Matching in the center, glue the game board patterns on a sheet of oak tag. Decorate the border around the game board, then laminate. Reproduce, color, laminate, then cut out the pawns and two sets of game cards. Measure, cut, and tape a construction paper pocket to the back of the game board for pawn and game card storage.

To Play

Set up the game board on a table. Shuffle and place the game cards, face down, next to the game board. Each player, in turn, draws a card and moves his or her pawn to the matching lowercase alphabet picture space. Players place used cards in a discard pile. When all cards have been drawn, reshuffle the discard pile for children to continue playing. Play continues until each player reaches the buttons at The End.

Pawns

Find Bear's Buttons Game Cards

Find Bear's Buttons

Bear lost his buttons. Follow the trail to find them.

Find Bear's Buttons Game Board

The End

After Reading JACK AND THE BEANSTALK

Jack's Letter Beanstalk

Reproduce, color, and cut out two beanstalk patterns (p. 31). Glue each beanstalk inside a folder. Write "Jack's Letter Beanstalk" on the front. Then reproduce, color, cut out and glue leaves and a Jack pattern (p. 27) to the front of the folder. Glue a storage envelope to the back of the folder. Reproduce leaf patterns (p. 32), program with upper and lowercase letters, and cut out. Children practice matching upper and lowercase leaves on the beanstalk. Make additional beanstalks to practice more letters.

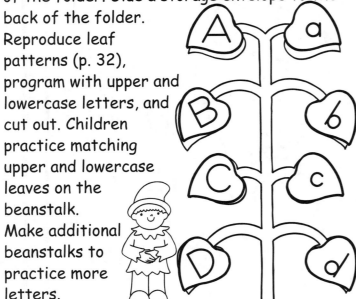

Alphabet Cows

Reproduce and program 26 cows (p. 33) with alphabet pictures (p. 4). Color, laminate, and cut out the cows. Reproduce, program, laminate, and cut out 52 cow spots (p. 33) with upper and lowercase letters. Write "Alphabet Cows" on the front of a large envelope. Then color, cut out, and glue a cow on the front of the envelope. Children sort and place matching upper and lowercase spots on each alphabet picture cow.

Goose Eggs Alphabet

Reproduce and cut out alphabet eggs (p. 30). Reproduce, program, cut out, and glue 26 lowercase letter nests to the inside of a folder. Write "Goose Eggs Alphabet" on the front of the folder. Decorate the front of the folder with goose (p. 27), egg, and nest (p. 30) cutouts. Tape an envelope to the back of the folder to store the alphabet eggs. Children sort and place uppercase eggs on the matching lowercase nests.

Alphabet Beans For Jack

Reproduce and cut out green alphabet beans (p. 29). Reproduce, program, cut out, and glue 26 lowercase letter bean bags (p. 29) to the inside of a folder. Write "Alphabet Beans for Jack" on the front of the folder. Decorate the front of the folder with Jack and bean cutouts. Tape an envelope to the back of the folder to store the alphabet beans. Children sort and place uppercase beans on the matching lowercase bean bags.

Goose and Jack Patterns

Provide children with craft sticks, crayons, markers, scissors, and glue to make stick puppets.

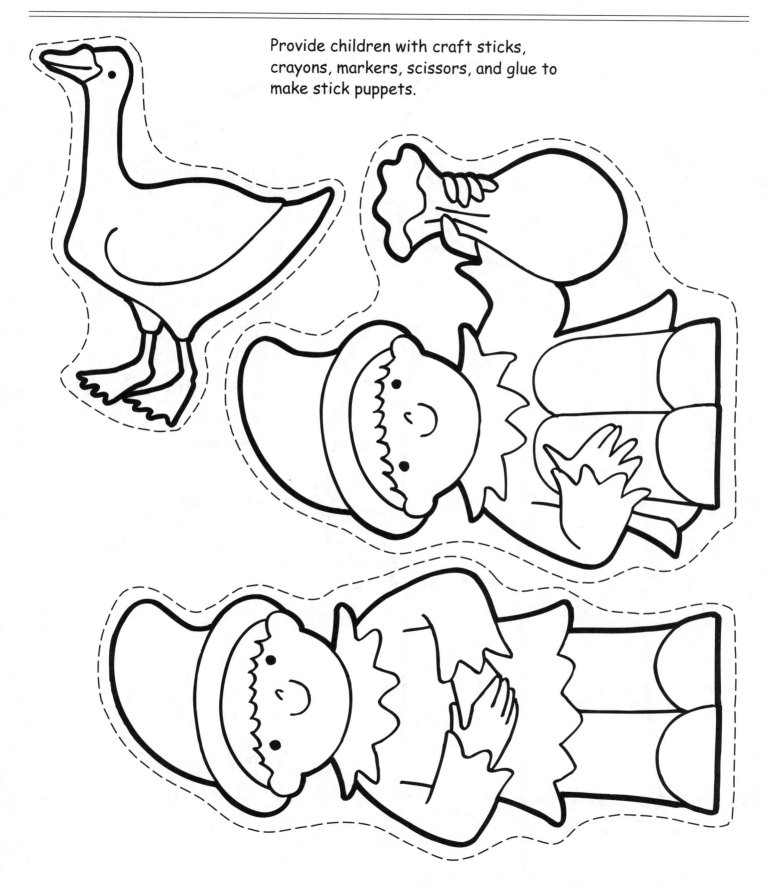

Giant and Harp

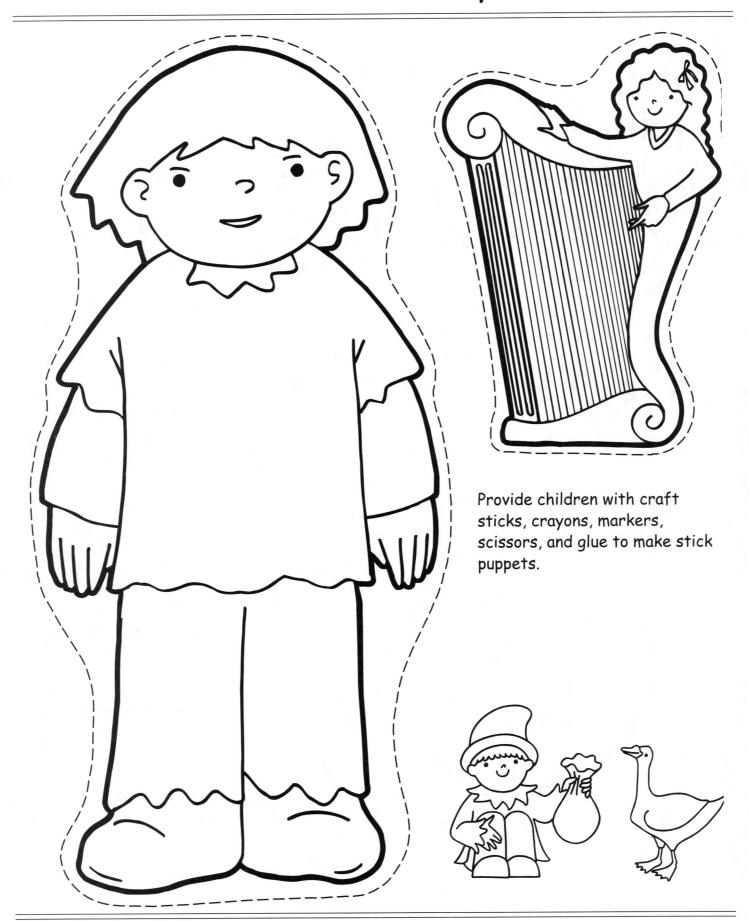

Provide children with craft sticks, crayons, markers, scissors, and glue to make stick puppets.

Alphabet Beans and Bean Bags

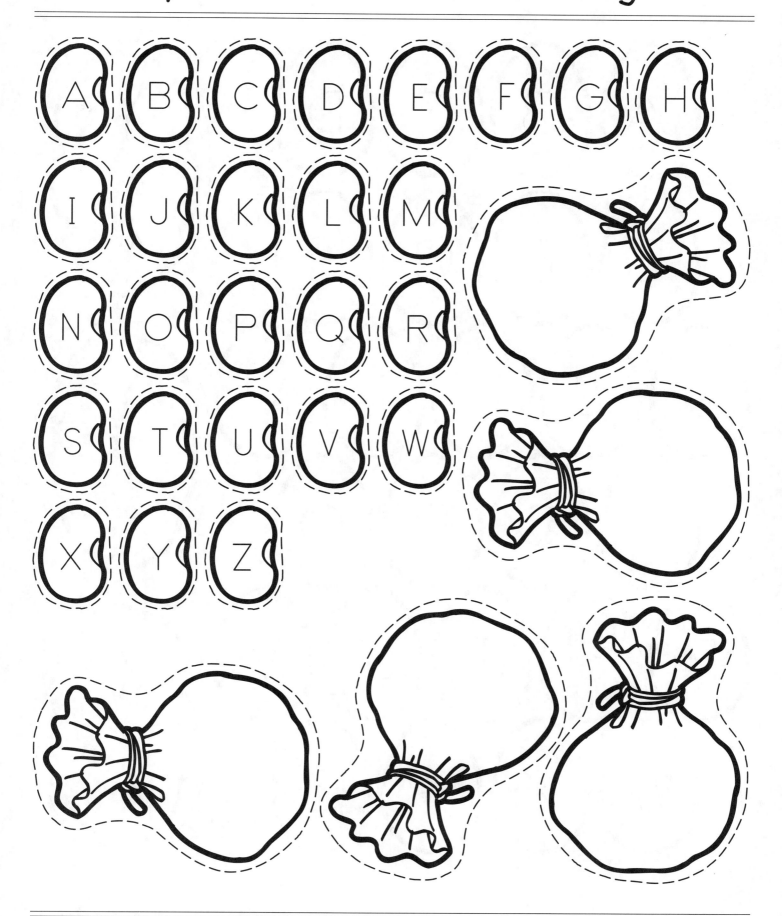

Alphabet Eggs and Nests

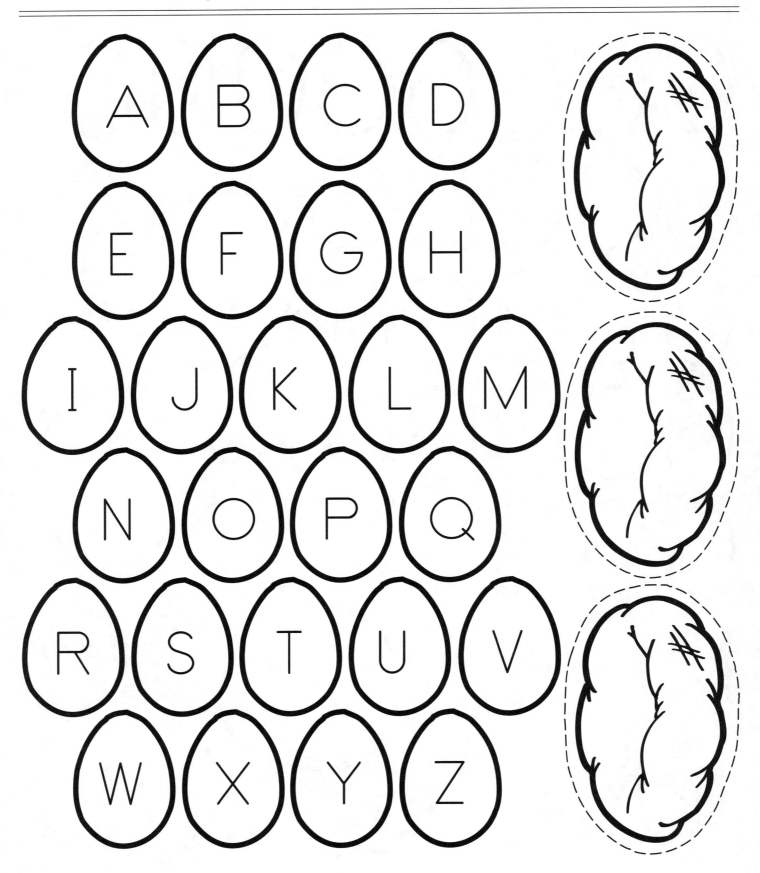

Beanstalk

Reproduce seven beanstalk patterns to make an upper and lowercase alphabet beanstalk. Overlap and glue the stalks together to form Jack's beanstalk.

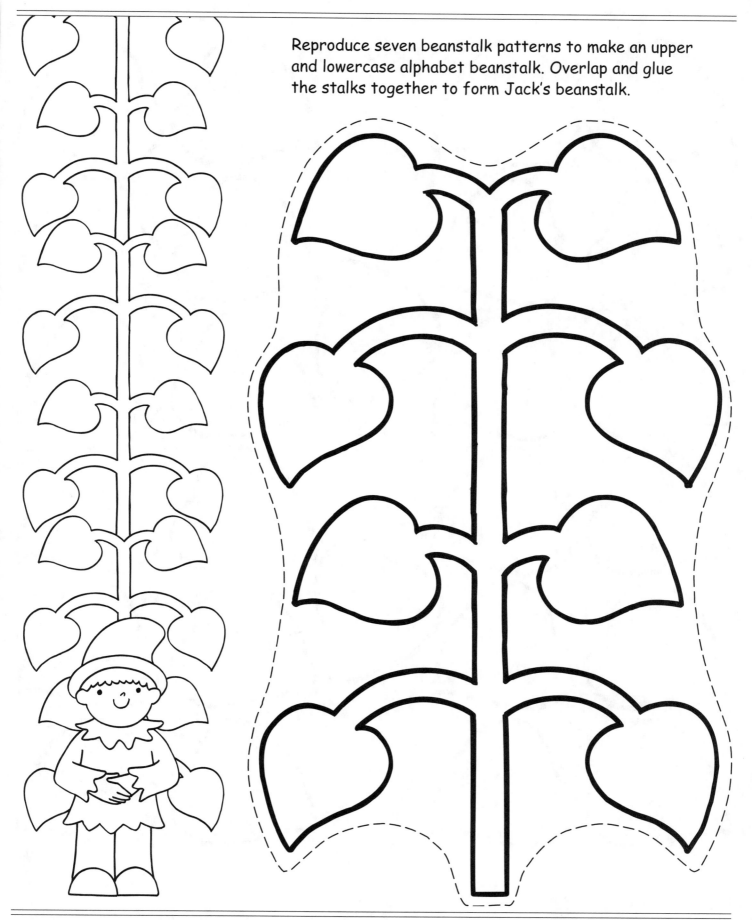

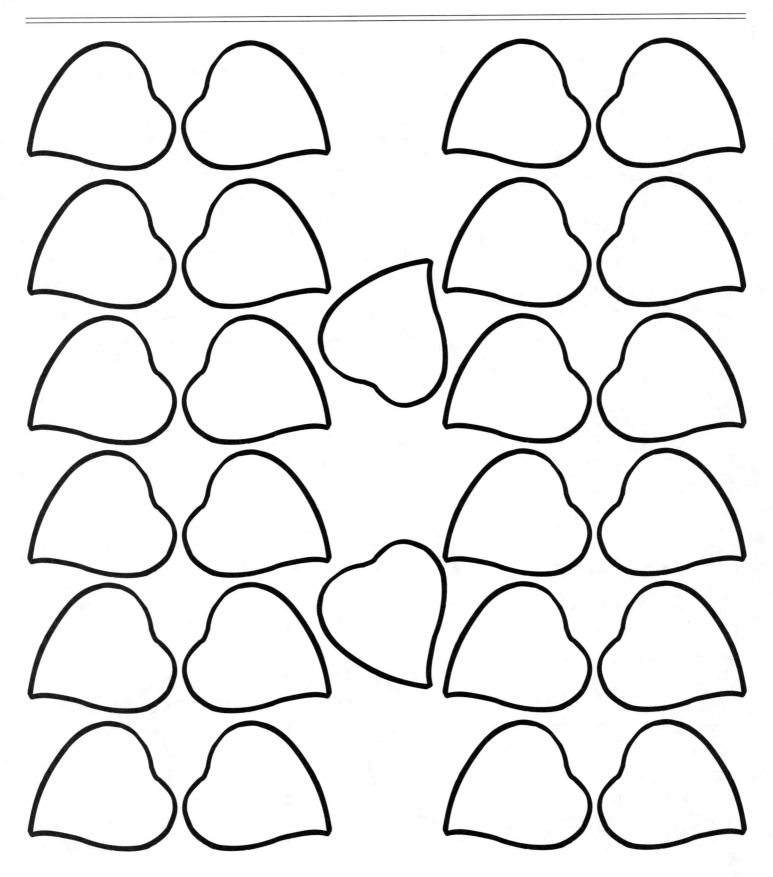

Cows and Spots

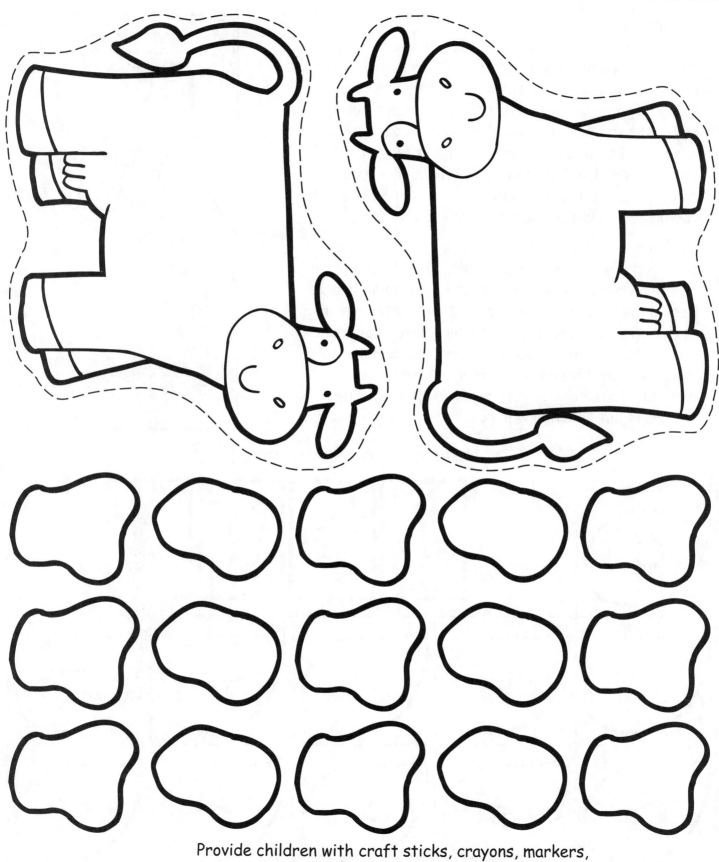

Provide children with craft sticks, crayons, markers,
scissors, and glue to make stick puppets.

Let's Play *Down the Beanstalk*

Assembly

Reproduce, color, and cut out the "Down the Beanstalk" game board patterns. Overlap and match the game board halves at the center (vertically). Glue the game board patterns on a sheet of oak tag. Decorate the border around the game board, then laminate. Reproduce, color, laminate, then cut out the pawns and two sets of game cards. Measure, cut, and tape a construction paper pocket to the back of the game board for pawn and game card storage.

To Play

Set up the game board on a table. Shuffle and place the game cards, face down, next to the game board. Each player, in turn, draws a card and moves his or her pawn to the space with the matching uppercase letter. Players place used cards in a discard pile. When all cards have been drawn, reshuffle the discard pile for children to continue playing. Play continues until each player reaches Jack's house at The End.

Pawns and Game cards

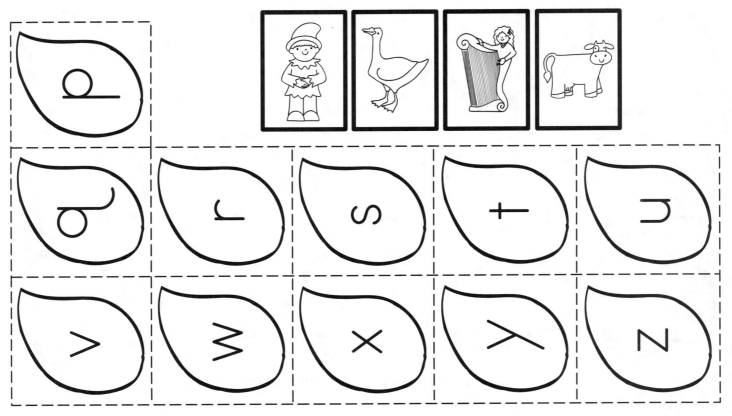

Down the Beanstalk Game Board

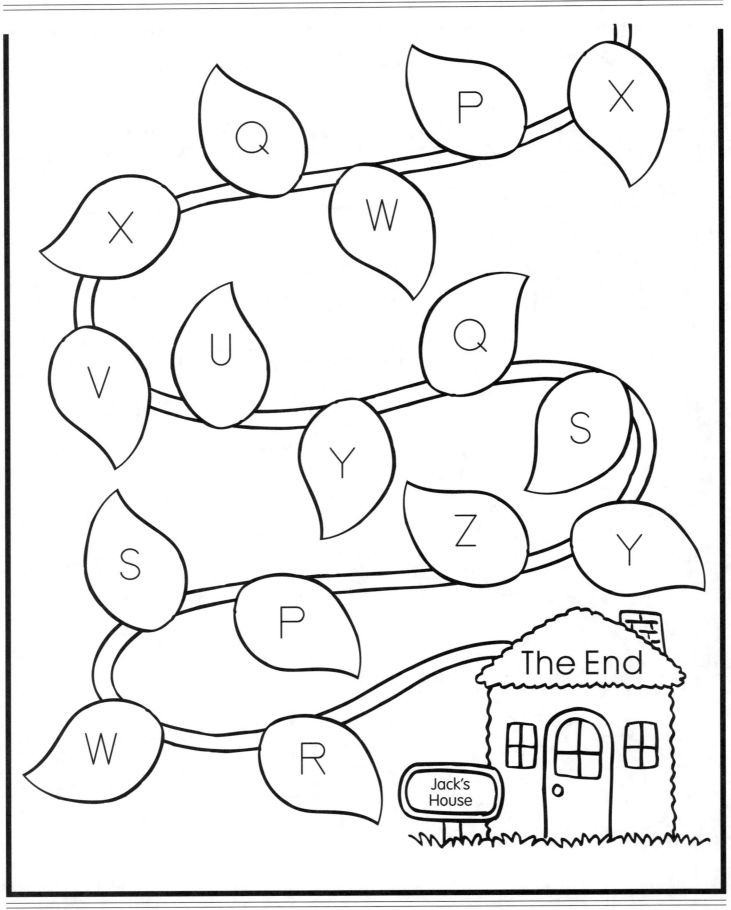

36

Flowers For Mary

Prepare a work station with construction paper, crayons, markers, scissors, and glue. Reproduce Mary and Hat patterns (p. 38) for children to color and cut out. Reproduce the same number of Flower Pots and flowers (p. 38) as letters in each child's name. (For Mary, reproduce four pots and flowers.) Have children glue the patterns on a sheet of construction paper. Help children write their names on the flower pots.

Flower Pot Match

Reproduce and program 26 flower pots with alphabet pictures (p. 4). Color, cut out, and glue the flower pots on sentence strips. Attach the sentence strips along the bottom of a display board. Draw a green stem above each pot. Glue a Velcro fastener square at the top of each stem. Reproduce, color, and cut out daisies (p. 39). Attach a Velcro fastener square to the back of each flower. Place the flowers in a basket beside the display board. Children draw and attach letter flowers to the matching pots.

Water the Alphabet Garden

Reproduce 26 flower pots (p. 38), a set of tulips (p. 40), and two copies of the watering can cards (p. 41). Program the watering can cards with uppercase letters. Color, cut out, assemble, and glue the flowers and pots on the inside of a folder. Write "Water the Alphabet Garden" on the front of the folder. Decorate the folder with flower cutouts. Attach an envelope to the back of the folder for watering can card storage. Children place watering can cards on matching lowercase flowers.

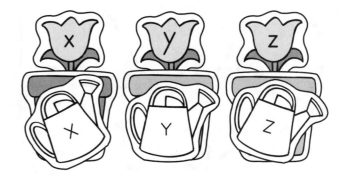

Alphabet Bouquets

Enlarge and reproduce three sets of daisies or tulips. Program one set with alphabet pictures (p. 4). Have each child choose a matching set of alphabet flowers to color and cut out. Provide each child with three different length plastic straws. Help children tape a flower to each straw. Then help each child tie a bow around each alphabet bouquet. Display the bouquets in flower vases around the room.

Mary, Hat, and Flower Pots

Provide children with craft sticks, crayons, markers, scissors, and glue to make stick puppets.

Daisies

Prepare a work station with construction paper daisies, crayons, markers, scissors, yarn, and hole punches for children to make daisy necklaces.

Tulips

Prepare a work station with construction paper tulips, crayons, markers, scissors, yarn, and hole punches for children to make tulip necklaces.

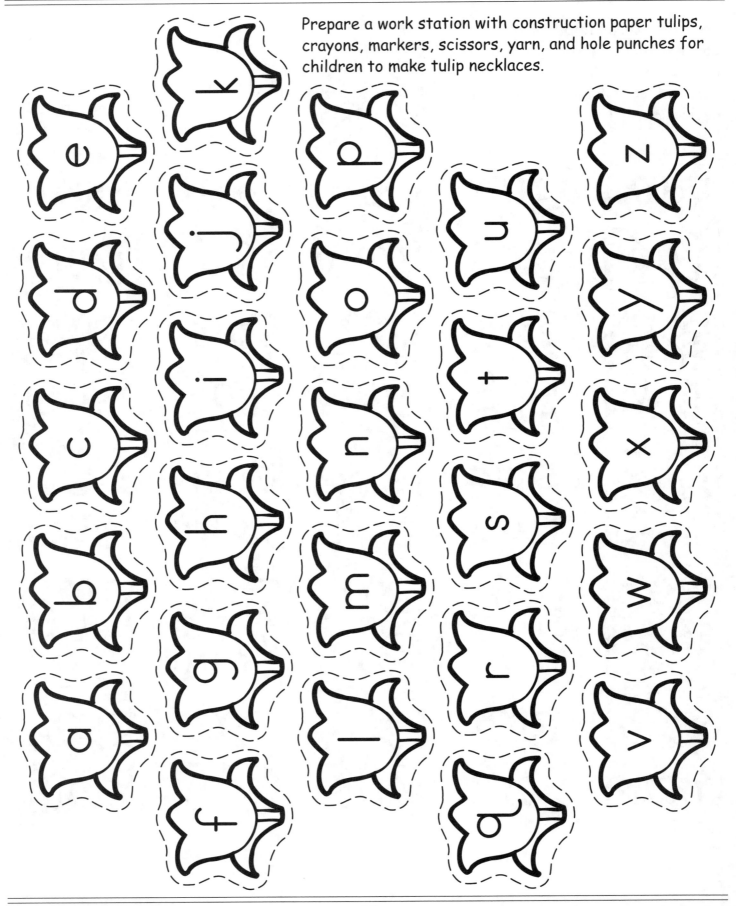

Watering Can Cards

Prepare a work station with construction paper watering cans, crayons, markers, scissors, yarn, and hole punches for children to make watering can garlands.

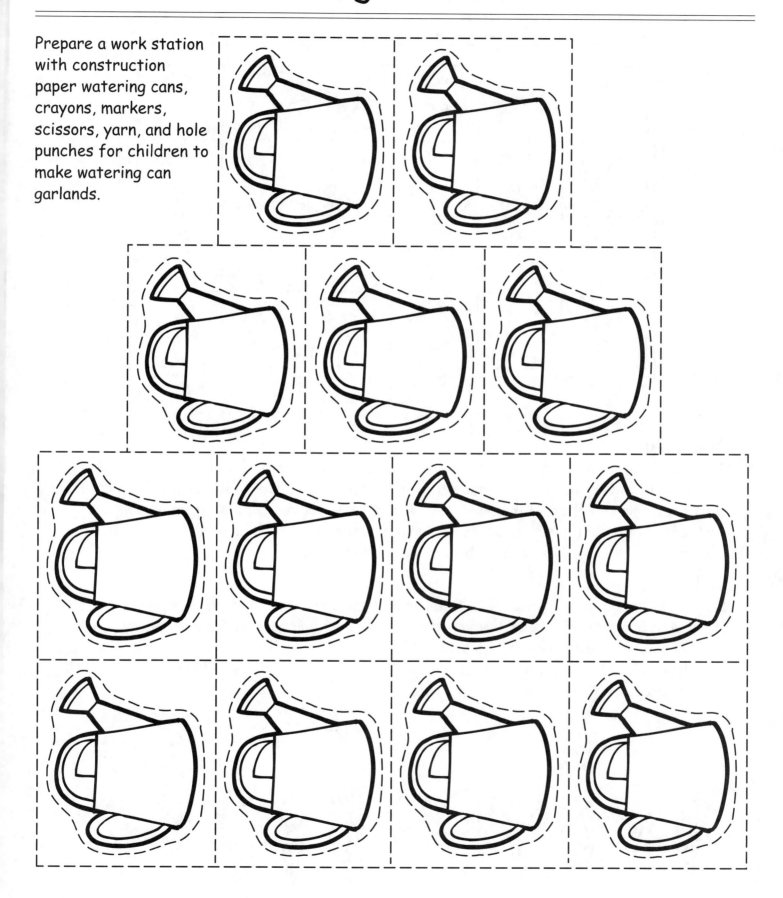

Let's Play *How Does Your Garden Grow?*

Assembly

Reproduce, color, and cut out the "How Does Your Garden Grow?" match board patterns. Matching in the center, glue the match board patterns on a sheet of oak tag. Decorate the border around the match board, then laminate. Reproduce and program two sets of lowercase consonant game cards. Color, laminate, then cut apart the cards. Tape an envelope to the back of the game board for card storage.

To Play

Set up the match board on a table. Shuffle and place the game cards, face down, next to the match board. Each player, in turn, draws a card and places the card on the matching uppercase consonant space on the board. If a card has already been placed on the board, the player places it in a discard pile and the next player takes a turn. Play continues until all the spaces on the match board are filled.

How Does Your Garden Grow? Match Board

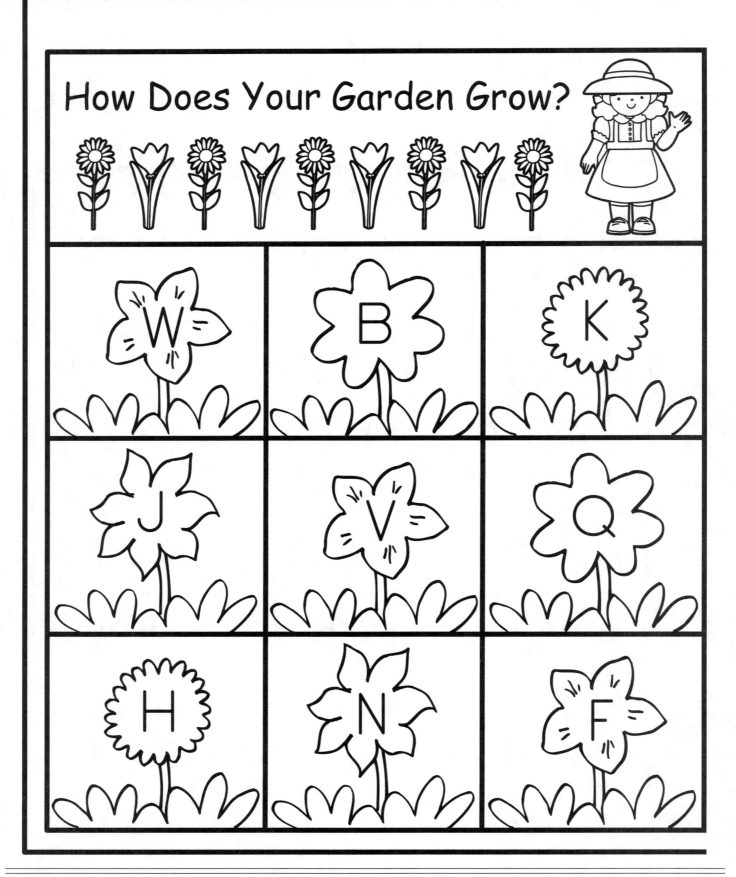

How Does Your Garden Grow?

How Does Your Garden Grow? Match Board

Alphabet Boots For Puss

Reproduce, program, color, and cut out 26 sets of boots (p. 48) with upper and lowercase letters. Write "Alphabet Boots For Puss" on the front of an envelope.
Reproduce, color, cut out, and glue a Puss 'n Boots pattern (p. 47) on the front of the envelope. Children place matching upper and lowercase boots on Puss 'n Boots.

Alphabet Cats

Reproduce 27 cat patterns (p. 48) for each child to color and cut out. Have children write a matching upper and lowercase letter on each of 26 cats. Write "Alphabet Cats" on each child's remaining cat cutout to use as a cover.
Punch a hole at the top of each child's alphabet cats. Stack the cats in alphabetical order and secure with a brass fastener to form a booklet. Children can decorate their covers.

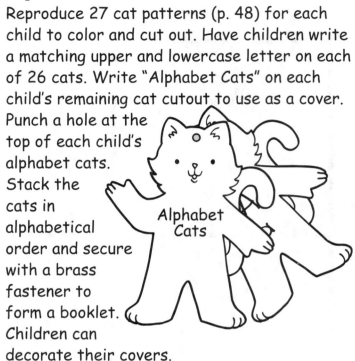

Gift Sack Match

Reproduce and cut apart the alphabet bird and rabbit gifts (pp. 49-50). Reproduce, program, cut out, and glue 26 sacks (p. 47) with an alphabet picture (p. 4) to the inside of a folder. Write "Gift Sack Match" on the front of a folder. Decorate the front of the folder with a Puss 'n Boots cutout holding a sack. Tape an envelope to the back of the folder to store the bird and rabbit cards. Children sort and place bird and rabbit cards on each matching alphabet picture sack.

Color a Calico Cat

Enlarge and draw shapes on a cat pattern (p. 48) as shown here. Create a color-by-letter legend at the bottom of the page. Then program each shape with a letter. Reproduce a cat for each child to color and cut out. Write each child's name on the back of his or her cat. Mount cats on a Display entitled "Color a Calico Cat."

Puss 'n Boots and Sacks

Provide children with craft
sticks, crayons, markers,
scissors, and glue to make
stick puppets.

47

Boots and Cat

Provide children with craft
sticks, crayons, markers,
scissors, and glue to make
stick puppets.

Alphabet Bird Gifts

Prepare a work station with construction paper birds, crayons, markers, scissors, yarn, and hole punches for children to make alphabet bird garlands.

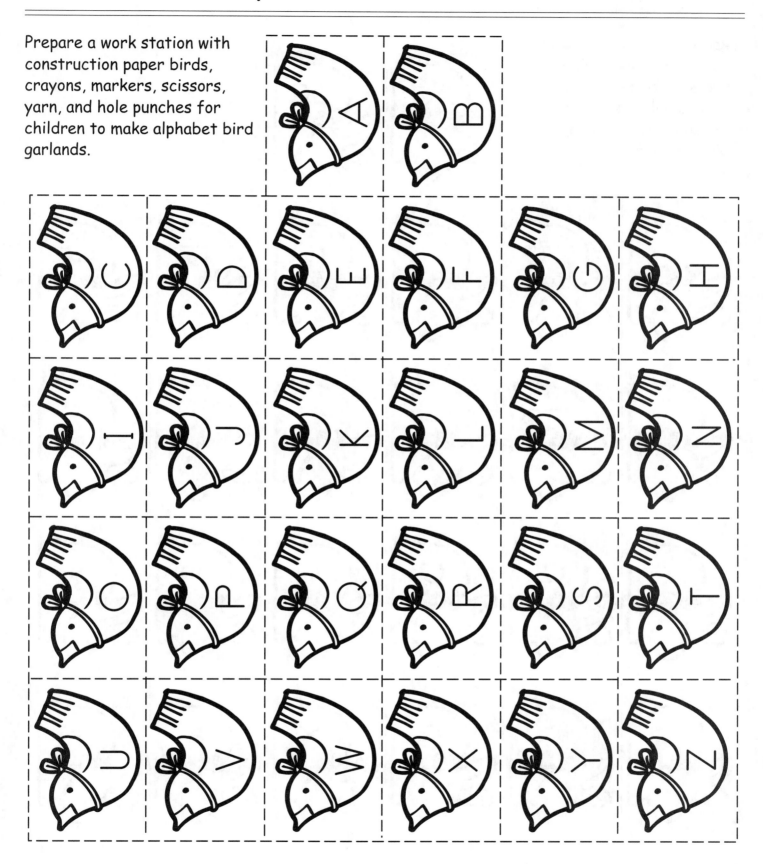

Alphabet Rabbit Gifts

Prepare a work station with construction paper rabbits, crayons, markers, scissors, yarn, and hole punches for children to make alphabet rabbit garlands.

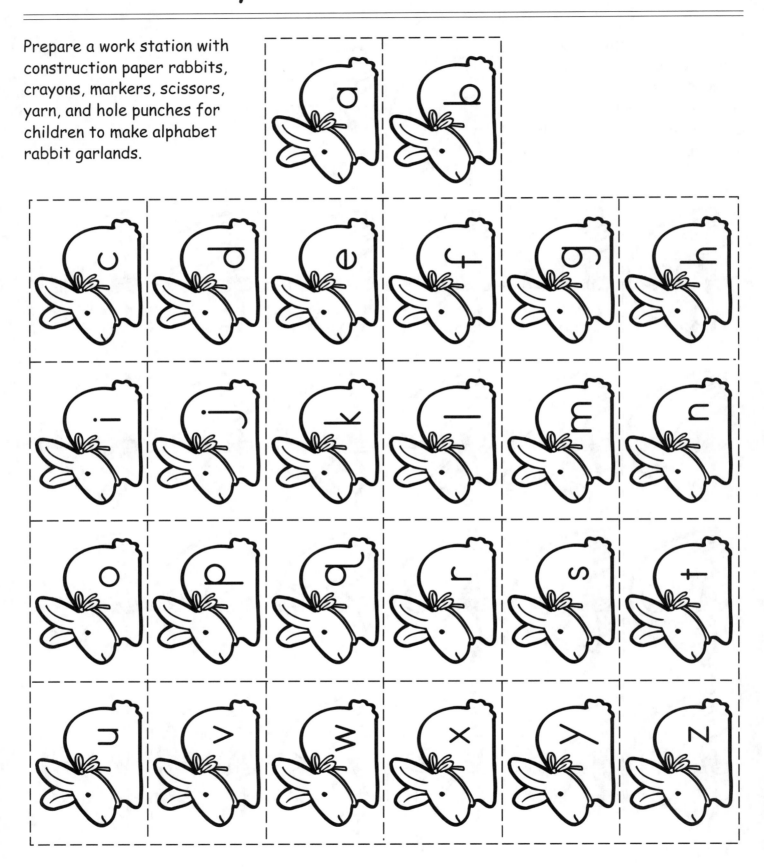

Let's Play *Journey to the Castle*

Assembly

Reproduce, color, and cut out the "Journey to the Castle" game board patterns. Overlap and match the game board halves at the center. Glue the game board patterns on a sheet of oak tag. Decorate the border around the game board, then laminate. Reproduce, color, laminate, then cut out the pawns and two sets of game cards. Measure, cut, and tape a construction paper pocket to the back of the game board for pawn and game card storage.

To Play

Set up the game board on a table. Shuffle and place the game cards, face down, next to the game board. Each player, in turn, draws a card and moves his or her pawn to the matching alphabet picture space. Players place used cards in a discard pile. When all cards have been drawn, reshuffle the discard pile for children to continue playing. Play continues until each player reaches the castle at The End.

Pawns

Journey to the Castle ~

Start

Journey to the Castle Game Board

The End

Journey to the Castle Game Cards

After Reading *OLD MOTHER HUBBARD*

Alphabet Bones

Reproduce, color, and cut out alphabet dog bowls and bones (pp. 58-59). Glue the dog bowls to the inside of a folder. Write "Alphabet Bones" on the front of the folder. Decorate the front of the folder with a Mother Hubbard (p. 56) and dog (p. 57) cutout. Glue an envelope to the back of the folder to store the alphabet bones. Children sort and place lowercase bones on the matching uppercase dog bowls.

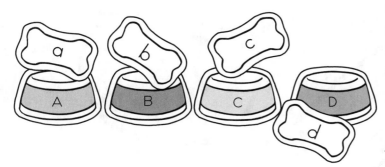

Stacking Alphabet Dishes

Reproduce and program 4 sets of dishes (p. 64) with upper and lowercase letters. Color, laminate, and cut out the dishes. Write "Stacking Alphabet Dishes" at the top of a large envelope. Decorate the folder with multicolored dishes. Children practice stacking the dishes in upper and lowercase alphabetical order.

Blowing Alphabet Bubbles

Reproduce and program 26 pipes (p. 60) with alphabet pictures (p. 4). Color, cut out, and glue the pipes on a large sheet of construction paper. Reproduce, program, color, and cut out 52 bubble patterns (p. 60) with upper and lowercase letters. Glue an envelope to the back of the construction paper for bubble storage. Children place letter bubbles on the matching alphabet picture pipes.

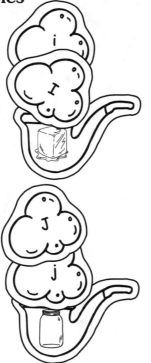

Alphabet Dogs

Reproduce 27 dog patterns (p. 57) for each child to color and cut out. Have children write a matching upper and lowercase letter on each of 26 dogs. Write "Alphabet Dogs" on each child's remaining dog cutout to use as a cover. Punch a hole at the top of each child's alphabet dogs. Stack the dogs in alphabetical order and secure with a brass fastener to form a booklet.

Mother Hubbard and Apron

Provide children with craft sticks, crayons, markers, scissors, and glue to make stick puppets.

Reproduce one Mother Hubbard and 26 apron patterns for children to make Mother Hubbard alphabet books.

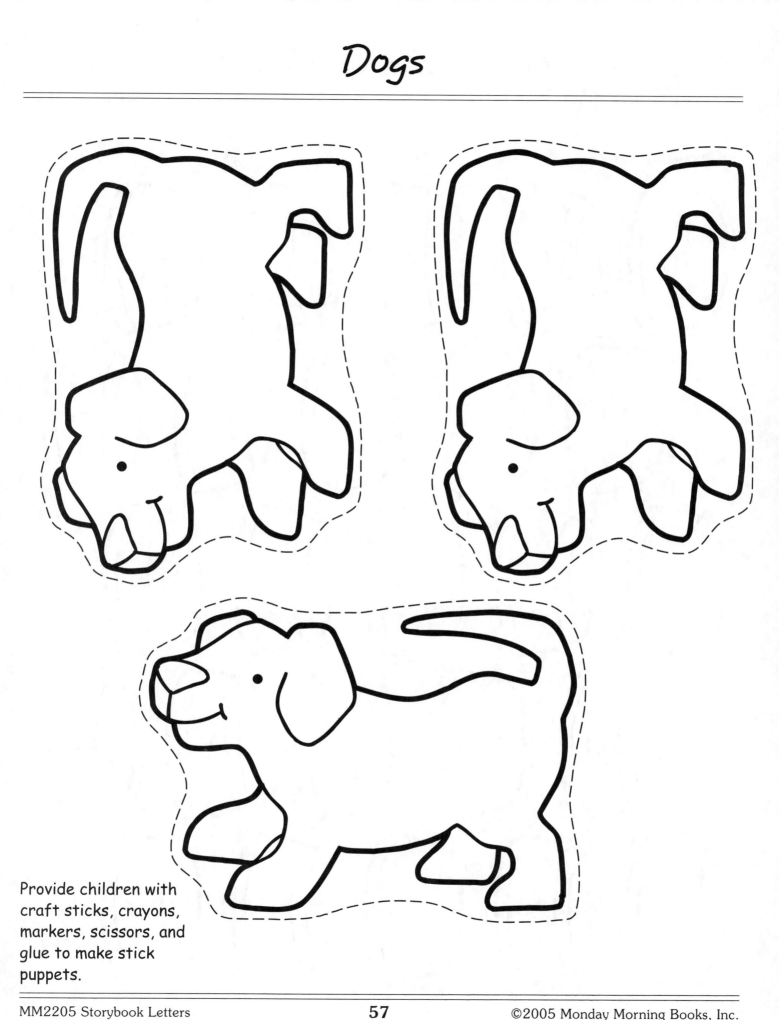

Provide children with craft sticks, crayons, markers, scissors, and glue to make stick puppets.

Alphabet Dog Bowls

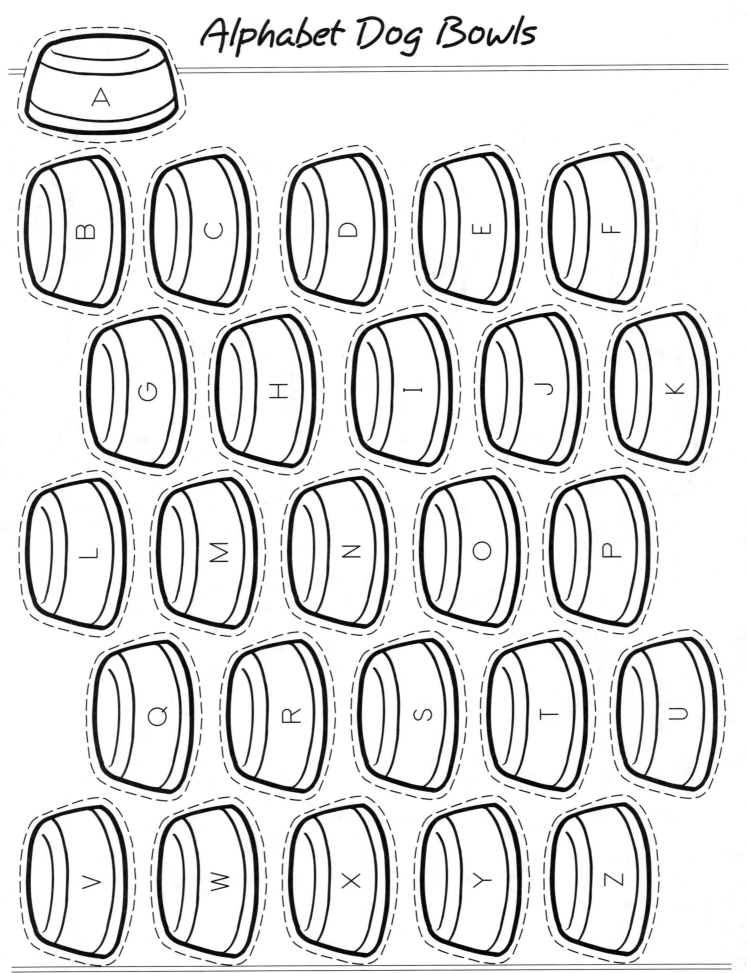

Alphabet Bones

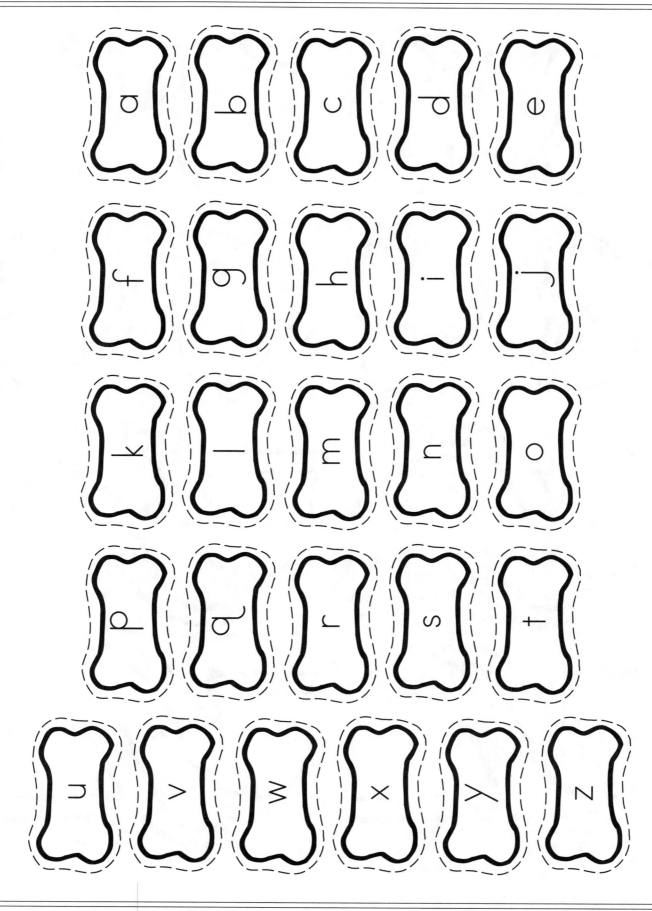

Pipes and Bubbles

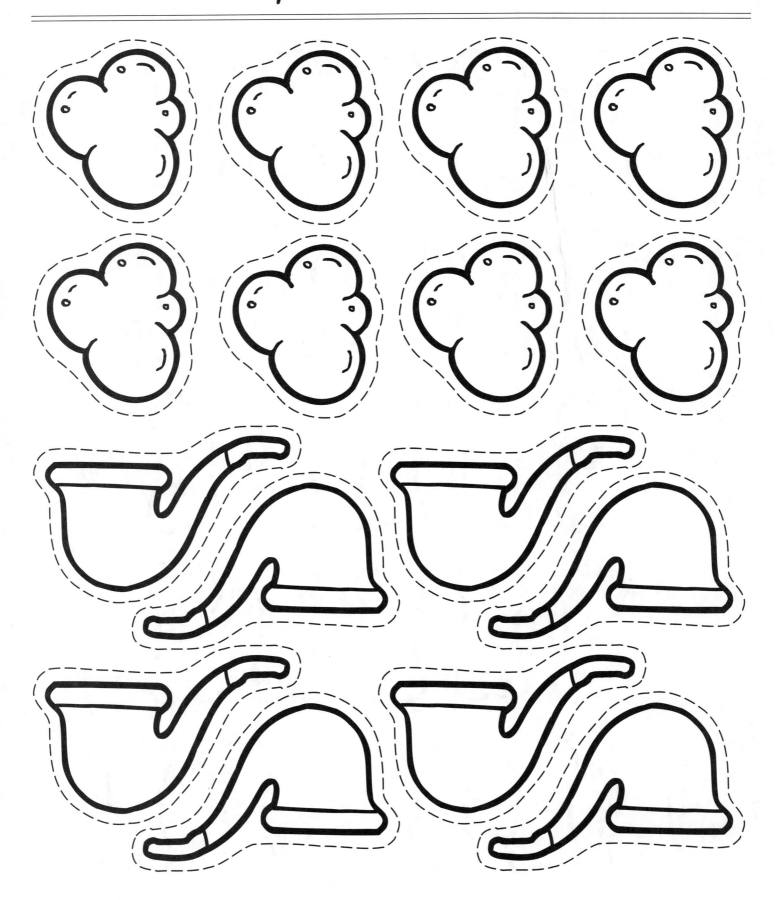

Let's Play *Mother Hubbard's Tic Tac Toe*

Assembly

Reproduce, color, cut out, and glue a "Mother Hubbard's Tic Tac Toe" board on a sheet of oak tag. Reproduce and program the teacups with two letters of the alphabet (five each). Measure, cut, and tape a construction paper pocket to the back of the oak tag for teacup storage.

To Play

Set up the match board on a table for two players. Each player chooses a set of teacup cards. In turn, each player places a teacup on the board. Each player has an opportunity to block the opponent from placing three cards in a row (vertically, horizontally, or diagonally). Play continues until one of the players has three cards in a row.

Note: Program teacups with the following letters for children to practice recognizing the differences: D and B, d and b, M and W, m and w, U and V, u and v, O and Q, p and q.

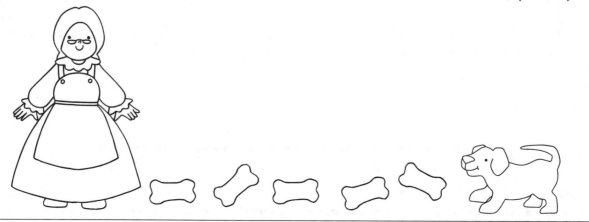

Mother Hubbard's Tic Tac Toe

Mother Hubbard's Tic Tac Toe

Tea Cups

Dishes

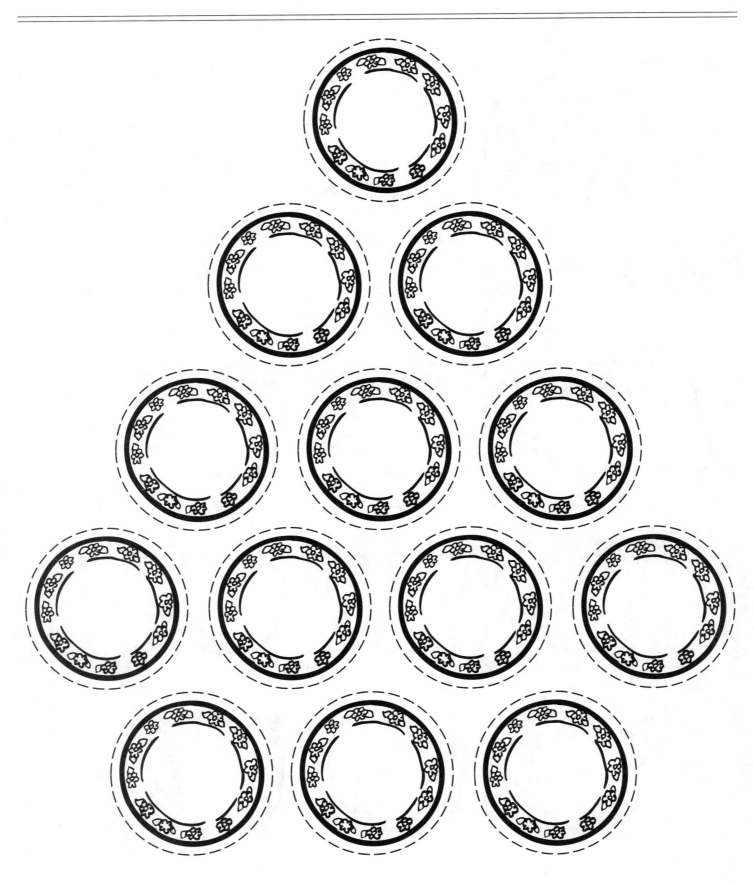